Presented to:

....

By:

....

Date:

....

The Bible
Promise Book®

. . . .

500
Scriptures
❯❯ for ❮❮
COURAGEOUS
Girls

The Bible Promise Book®

500 Scriptures

for

COURAGEOUS Girls

Written and Compiled by
Janice Thompson

BARBOUR kidz
A Division of Barbour Publishing

Published by Barbour Publishing, Inc., 1810 Barbour Drive, Uhrichsville, Ohio 44683, www.barbourbooks.com

Our mission is to inspire the world with the life-changing message of the Bible.

Member of the
Evangelical Christian
Publishers Association

Contents

~~~~~~~~~~~~~~

Introduction

~~~~~~~~~~~~

God's Word is filled with rich and wonderful promises for you, His courageous girl. You'll find many of
those promises in this little book.

Whether you're struggling with fear, jealousy,
hurt, or selfishness, the scripture selections in this
book will remind you of God's promise that He is
never far away. No matter what struggles you're up
against, there's something here for you.

If you're in a happy season, there's plenty to
keep you moving forward in your relationship with
Jesus.

Remember this, precious girl: people will sometimes break their promises, but God never will. If
His Word says it, you can count on it!

Be a God-Pleaser

Imagine you're at a fork in the road. If you take the path to the right, it will make God's heart happy; but if you take the path to the left, you'll fit in with your friends. So. . .which road do you take? It's not always easy to do the right thing, but pleasing God should *always* be the guide you use to make a difficult decision. Take that first step toward Him, courageous girl! He promises to guide you on the good path—every step of the way!

1

A man cannot please God unless he has faith. Anyone who comes to God must believe that He is. That one must also know that God gives what is promised to the one who keeps on looking for Him.
HEBREWS 11:6

2

Do you think I am trying to get the favor of men, or of God? If I were still trying to please men, I would not be a servant owned by Christ.
GALATIANS 1:10

3

God has allowed us to be trusted with the Good News. Because of this, we preach it to please God, not man. God tests and proves our hearts.

1 THESSALONIANS 2:4

4

When the ways of a man are pleasing to the Lord, He makes even those who hate him to be at peace with him.

PROVERBS 16:7

5

Those who do what their sinful old selves want to do cannot please God.

ROMANS 8:8

6

Do not act like the sinful people of the world. Let God change your life. First of all, let Him give you a new mind. Then you will know what God wants you to do. And the things you do will be good and pleasing and perfect.

ROMANS 12:2

7

*We will receive from Him whatever we ask
if we obey Him and do what He wants.*
1 John 3:22

8

*Remember to do good and help each other.
Gifts like this please God.*
Hebrews 13:16

9

*So if we stay here on earth or go home to Him,
we always want to please Him.*
2 Corinthians 5:9

10

*Then Peter and the missionaries said,
"We must obey God instead of men!"*
Acts 5:29

Be Brave and Courageous!

God will give you courage to face life's challenges!
You can be brave because of His power.

C: CAN. Use the words "I can" instead of
"I can't."
O: OBSTACLE. No obstacle is too big
when God is on your side!
U: UNIQUE. There's no one else on the
planet just like you.
R: RIGHTEOUS. God is righteous!
A: APPLE. You're the apple of the heavenly
Father's eye.
G: GREATNESS. God has amazing plans for
you, courageous girl!
E: ETERNITY. You belong to God. . .forever
and ever!

11

*The Lord is my rock, and my safe place, and the
One Who takes me out of trouble. My God is my
rock, in Whom I am safe. He is my safe-covering,
my saving strength, and my strong tower.*
PSALM 18:2

12

Do not fear, for I am with you. Do not be afraid,
for I am your God. I will give you strength, and
for sure I will help you. Yes, I will hold you up with
My right hand that is right and good.

ISAIAH 41:10

13

"For I am the Lord your God Who holds
your right hand, and Who says to you,
'Do not be afraid. I will help you.' "

ISAIAH 41:13

14

Do not be afraid of them who kill the body. They
are not able to kill the soul. But fear Him Who is
able to destroy both soul and body in hell.

MATTHEW 10:28

15

Watch and keep awake! Stand true to the Lord.
Keep on acting like men and be strong.
1 CORINTHIANS 16:13

16

"Be strong and have strength of heart.
Do not be afraid or shake with fear because
of them. For the Lord your God is the One Who
goes with you. He will be faithful to you.
He will not leave you alone."
DEUTERONOMY 31:6

17

The Lord is my light and the One Who saves me.
Whom should I fear? The Lord is the strength
of my life. Of whom should I be afraid?
PSALM 27:1

18

For God did not give us a spirit of fear. He gave us a spirit of power and of love and of a good mind.
2 Timothy 1:7

19

There is no fear in love. Perfect love puts fear out of our hearts. People have fear when they are afraid of being punished. The man who is afraid does not have perfect love.
1 John 4:18

20

Then David said to his son Solomon, "Be strong. Have strength of heart, and do it. Do not be afraid or troubled, for the Lord God, my God, is with you. He will not stop helping you. He will not leave you until all the work of the house of the Lord is finished."
1 Chronicles 28:20

Choices

Choices, choices. . .so many choices! Everywhere you look, there are things to choose. Should you have the burger or a pepperoni pizza? Should you choose a healthy salad? Should you obey your parents—or not? Should you be nice to the mean girl? Should you talk to your friends about Jesus or let someone else do that? As you read the following biblical promises, remember: the choices you make today could have a "forever" impact!

21

"Go in through the narrow door. The door is wide and the road is easy that leads to hell. Many people are going through that door. But the door is narrow and the road is hard that leads to life that lasts forever. Few people are finding it."
MATTHEW 7:13–14

22

*There is a way which looks right to a man,
but its end is the way of death.*
PROVERBS 14:12

23

*The mind of a man plans his way,
but the Lord shows him what to do.*
PROVERBS 16:9

24

*There are many plans in a man's heart,
but it is the Lord's plan that will stand.*
PROVERBS 19:21

25

*Your ears will hear a word behind you, saying,
"This is the way, walk in it," whenever you
turn to the right or to the left.*

Isaiah 30:21

26

*Christian brothers, keep your minds thinking
about whatever is true, whatever is respected,
whatever is right, whatever is pure, whatever can
be loved, and whatever is well thought of. If there
is anything good and worth giving thanks for,
think about these things.*

Philippians 4:8

27

*My son, do not forget my teaching. Let your
heart keep my words. For they will add to you
many days and years of life and peace.*

Proverbs 3:1–2

28

You have never been tempted to sin in any different way than other people. God is faithful. He will not allow you to be tempted more than you can take. But when you are tempted, He will make a way for you to keep from falling into sin.

1 Corinthians 10:13

29

If you do not have wisdom, ask God for it. He is always ready to give it to you and will never say you are wrong for asking.

James 1:5

30

The way of a fool is right in his own eyes, but a wise man listens to good teaching.

Proverbs 12:15

Church Life

Some people think that church is a building where people go to worship. But get this: the church is really the *people*, not the building! We, "the church," come together to praise God, to learn more about His Word, and to encourage each other in our faith. According to God's Word, church is meant to be powerful and fun! Together, God's people can grow, grow, grow!

31

Let us not stay away from church meetings. Some people are doing this all the time. Comfort each other as you see the day of His return coming near.
HEBREWS 10:25

32

"For where two or three are gathered together in My name, there I am with them."
MATTHEW 18:20

33

Let the teaching of Christ and His words keep on living in you. These make your lives rich and full of wisdom. Keep on teaching and helping each other. Sing the Songs of David and the church songs and the songs of heaven with hearts full of thanks to God.
COLOSSIANS 3:16

34

They were faithful in listening to the teaching of the missionaries. They worshiped and prayed and ate the Lord's supper together.
ACTS 2:42

35

*There are many people who belong to Christ.
And yet, we are one body which is Christ's.
We are all different but we depend on each other.*
ROMANS 12:5

36

*"And I tell you that you are Peter. On this rock
I will build My church. The powers of hell will
not be able to have power over My church."*
MATTHEW 16:18

37

*Christ gave gifts to men. He gave to some the
gift to be missionaries, some to be preachers,
others to be preachers who go from town to
town. He gave others the gift to be church
leaders and teachers. These gifts help His people
work well for Him. And then the church which is
the body of Christ will be made strong.*
EPHESIANS 4:11–12

38

Keep a careful watch over yourselves and over the church. The Holy Spirit has made you its leaders. Feed and care for the church of God. He bought it with His own blood.
ACTS 20:28

39

On the first day of the week we met together to eat the Lord's supper. Paul talked to them. He thought he would leave the next day, so he kept on talking until twelve o'clock at night.
ACTS 20:7

40

Let us hold on to the hope we say we have and not be changed. We can trust God that He will do what He promised. Let us help each other to love others and to do good. Let us not stay away from church meetings. Some people are doing this all the time. Comfort each other as you see the day of His return coming near.
HEBREWS 10:23–25

Disappointment

When something you had expected to happen doesn't, you're disappointed—especially if it was something you were really looking forward to. Does God even care that your heart is broken? Oh, but He does! And that's a promise from His Word! When you're disappointed, He will bring hope, courage, and healing. Trust Him today with anything that has disappointed you.

41

"Do not let your heart be troubled. You have put your trust in God, put your trust in Me also."
JOHN 14:1

42

Give all your cares to the Lord and He will give you strength. He will never let those who are right with Him be shaken.

Psalm 55:22

43

" 'For I know the plans I have for you,' says the Lord, 'plans for well-being and not for trouble, to give you a future and a hope.' "

Jeremiah 29:11

44

Is anyone among you suffering? He should pray. Is anyone happy? He should sing songs of thanks to God.

James 5:13

45

He who lives in the safe place of the Most High will be in the shadow of the All-powerful. I will say to the Lord, "You are my safe and strong place, my God, in Whom I trust."

PSALM 91:1–2

46

"Do not fear, for I am with you. Do not be afraid, for I am your God. I will give you strength, and for sure I will help you. Yes, I will hold you up with My right hand that is right and good."

ISAIAH 41:10

47

So comfort each other and make each other strong as you are already doing.

1 THESSALONIANS 5:11

48

*"Peace I leave with you. My peace I give to you.
I do not give peace to you as the world gives.
Do not let your hearts be troubled or afraid."*
JOHN 14:27

49

*After you have suffered for awhile, God
Himself will make you perfect. He will
keep you in the right way. He will give you
strength. He is the God of all loving-favor
and has called you through Christ Jesus to
share His shining-greatness forever.*
1 PETER 5:10

50

*"I have told you these things so you
may have peace in Me. In the world you
will have much trouble. But take hope!
I have power over the world!"*
JOHN 16:33

Doing What's Right

~~~~~~~~~~~~~~~

Sometimes it seems easier to disobey, doesn't it? For example: Mom tells you to clean your room, but you don't feel like it. . .so you end up playing a video game instead. An hour later, Mom comes into your room and sees you haven't cleaned up one thing. And now you're grounded *and* stuck in your room until it's clean. Obedience, even when it's hard, is always the right thing, courageous girl! Even better, God promises to honor your obedience.

51

"If you love Me, you will do what I say."
JOHN 14:15

52

*"And why do you call Me,
'Lord, Lord,' but do not do what I say?"*
LUKE 6:46

53

*Jesus said, "The one who loves Me will obey
My teaching. My Father will love him. We will
come to him and live with him."*
JOHN 14:23

54

Adam did not obey God, and many people become sinners through him. Christ obeyed God and makes many people right with Himself.
ROMANS 5:19

55

"Not everyone who says to me, 'Lord, Lord,' will go into the holy nation of heaven. The one who does the things My Father in heaven wants him to do will go into the holy nation of heaven."
MATTHEW 7:21

56

Love means that we should live by obeying His Word. From the beginning He has said in His Word that our hearts should be full of love.
2 JOHN 6

57

Obey the Word of God. If you hear only and do not act, you are only fooling yourself.
JAMES 1:22

58

Samuel said, "Is the Lord pleased as much with burnt gifts as He is when He is obeyed? See, it is better to obey than to give gifts. It is better to listen than to give the fat of rams."
1 SAMUEL 15:22

59

"If you are willing and obey,
you will eat the best of the land."
ISAIAH 1:19

60

Then Peter and the missionaries said,
"We must obey God instead of men!"
ACTS 5:29

Faith to Believe

It takes strong faith to believe in something you can't see with your eyes or hear with your ears. That's why some people have such a hard time believing in God—they can't see Him or touch Him to have proof that He's real. Courageous girl, God wants you to strengthen your faith. Just ask Him, and He'll help you "see" that He's your Master, Creator, Savior, and Friend!

61

"All things you ask for in prayer, you will receive if you have faith."
MATTHEW 21:22

62

Now faith is being sure we will get what we hope for. It is being sure of what we cannot see.
HEBREWS 11:1

63

Jesus said to her, "Did I not say that if you would believe, you would see the shining-greatness of God?"
JOHN 11:40

64

For by His loving-favor you have been saved from the punishment of sin through faith. It is not by anything you have done. It is a gift of God. It is not given to you because you worked for it. If you could work for it, you would be proud.
EPHESIANS 2:8–9

65

The followers said to the Lord, "Give us more faith."
LUKE 17:5

66

If you do not have wisdom, ask God for it. He is always ready to give it to you and will never say you are wrong for asking. You must have faith as you ask Him. You must not doubt. Anyone who doubts is like a wave which is pushed around by the sea. Such a man will get nothing from the Lord. The man who has two ways of thinking changes in everything he does.
JAMES 1:5–8

67

Jesus said to them, "Because you have so little faith. For sure, I tell you, if you have faith as a mustard seed, you will say to this mountain, 'Move from here to over there,' and it would move over. You will be able to do anything."
MATTHEW 17:20

68

I have fought a good fight. I have finished the work I was to do. I have kept the faith.
2 TIMOTHY 4:7

69

"We believe and know You are the Christ. You are the Son of the Living God."
JOHN 6:69

70

Jesus said to them, "Have faith in God. For sure, I tell you, a person may say to this mountain, 'Move from here into the sea.' And if he does not doubt, but believes that what he says will be done, it will happen. Because of this, I say to you, whatever you ask for when you pray, have faith that you will receive it. Then you will get it."
MARK 11:22–24

Family Matters!

God is so happy when kids and parents love each other and live together peacefully. He wants your family relationships to be positive and joy-filled! No matter what you're going through—even if your family is struggling—God can help make things better. That's a promise! Do what's right (love and obey your parents), and then watch as God honors your obedience. Exciting things lie ahead for those who trust and obey His Word!

71

"Honor your father and your mother, so your life may be long in the land the Lord your God gives you."
EXODUS 20:12

72

Bring up a child by teaching him the way he should go, and when he is old he will not turn away from it.
PROVERBS 22:6

73

Children, obey your parents in everything. The Lord is pleased when you do.
COLOSSIANS 3:20

74

*Anyone who does not take care of his family
and those in his house has turned away
from the faith. He is worse than a person
who has never put his trust in Christ.*

1 Timothy 5:8

75

*Your wife will be like a vine with much
fruit within your house. Your children will
be like olive plants around your table.*

Psalm 128:3

76

*See, children are a gift from the Lord. The children
born to us are our special reward. The children
of a young man are like arrows in the hand of a
soldier. Happy is the man who has many of them.
They will not be put to shame when they speak
in the gate with those who hate them.*

Psalm 127:3–5

77

*My son, keep the teaching of your father, and do not
turn away from the teaching of your mother.*

Proverbs 6:20

78

Then Paul spoke the Word of God to him and his family. It was late at night, but the man who watched the prison took Paul and Silas in and washed the places on their bodies where they were hurt. Right then he and his family were baptized. He took Paul and Silas to his house and gave them food. He and all his family were full of joy for having put their trust in God.

ACTS 16:32–34

79

"Honor your father and your mother, as the Lord your God has told you. So your life may be long and it may go well with you in the land the Lord your God gives you."

DEUTERONOMY 5:16

80

I remember your true faith. It is the same faith your grandmother Lois had and your mother Eunice had. I am sure you have that same faith also.

2 TIMOTHY 1:5

Forgiveness

God will never ask you to do something that He isn't willing to do Himself. So when He tells you to forgive others, it's because He's already forgiven you for all of your sins. Forgiving those who hurt us isn't easy, but when we choose to do it, amazing things happen. And that's a promise from the Word of God! The act of forgiving will free you from bitterness and pain. It's critical to your faith journey, courageous girl!

81

You must be kind to each other. Think of the other person. Forgive other people just as God forgave you because of Christ's death on the cross.
EPHESIANS 4:32

82

"When you stand to pray, if you have anything against anyone, forgive him. Then your Father in heaven will forgive your sins also."
MARK 11:25

83

If we tell Him our sins, He is faithful and we can depend on Him to forgive us of our sins. He will make our lives clean from all sin.
1 JOHN 1:9

84

"If you do not forgive people their sins, your Father will not forgive your sins."
MATTHEW 6:15

85

Then Peter came to Jesus and said, "Lord, how many times may my brother sin against me and I forgive him, up to seven times?" Jesus said to him, "I tell you, not seven times but seventy times seven!"
MATTHEW 18:21–22

86

"Do not say what is wrong in other people's lives. Then other people will not say what is wrong in your life. Do not say someone is guilty. Then other people will not say you are guilty. Forgive other people and other people will forgive you."
LUKE 6:37

87

*Try to understand other people. Forgive each other.
If you have something against someone, forgive him.
That is the way the Lord forgave you.*
COLOSSIANS 3:13

88

*Tell your sins to each other. And pray for each
other so you may be healed. The prayer from the
heart of a man right with God has much power.*
JAMES 5:16

89

*"I say to you who hear Me, love those who work
against you. Do good to those who hate you."*
LUKE 6:27

90

*Because of the blood of Christ, we are
bought and made free from the punishment
of sin. And because of His blood, our sins are
forgiven. His loving-favor to us is so rich.*
EPHESIANS 1:7

Friendship

Where would we be without our friends? They lift us up when we're feeling down. They laugh with us when we're feeling silly. They give great advice and encourage us to do our very best. Some friendships are harder than others; there are a few girls (and boys) out there who are tougher to love. Choose your friends wisely, and they will help you to become a better human being. That, courageous girl, is God's promise to you!

91

A man who has friends must be a friend, but there is a friend who stays nearer than a brother.
PROVERBS 18:24

92

No one can have greater love than to give his life for his friends.
JOHN 15:13

93

Iron is made sharp with iron, and one man is made sharp by a friend.
PROVERBS 27:17

94

Two are better than one, because they have good pay for their work. For if one of them falls, the other can help him up. But it is hard for the one who falls when there is no one to lift him up.
ECCLESIASTES 4:9–10

95

Do not let anyone fool you. Bad people can make those who want to live good become bad.
1 CORINTHIANS 15:33

96

So comfort each other and make each other strong as you are already doing.
1 THESSALONIANS 5:11

97

*A bad man spreads trouble. One who hurts
people with bad talk separates good friends.*
PROVERBS 16:28

98

*He who walks with wise men will be wise,
but the one who walks with fools will be destroyed.*
PROVERBS 13:20

99

*Most of all, have a true love for each other.
Love covers many sins. Be happy to have
people stay for the night and eat with you.
God has given each of you a gift. Use it to help
each other. This will show God's loving-favor.*
1 PETER 4:8–10

100

*"Do for other people what you would
like to have them do for you."*
LUKE 6:31

Gentleness

Imagine you found a baby bird in your yard that had been separated from its mother. Would you snatch the bird up and run with him into the house to tell Mom? No. Instead you would very softly scoop him into your palm, and then take slow, careful steps toward the house. You wouldn't want to hurt him. And that's how God wants you to treat others, courageous girl—with that same gentle care. When we're gentle with those around us, they will sense our love.

101

They must not speak bad of anyone,
and they must not argue. They should
be gentle and kind to all people.
TITUS 3:2

102

Your heart should be holy and set apart for
the Lord God. Always be ready to tell everyone
who asks you why you believe as you do.
Be gentle as you speak and show respect.
1 PETER 3:15

103

A gentle answer turns away anger,
but a sharp word causes anger.
PROVERBS 15:1

104

You have also given me the covering that
saves me. Your right hand holds me up.
And Your care has made me great.
PSALM 18:35

105

But the fruit that comes from having the Holy
Spirit in our lives is: love, joy, peace, not giving
up, being kind, being good, having faith, being
gentle, and being the boss over our own desires.
The Law is not against these things.
GALATIANS 5:22–23

106

Men can make all kinds of animals and birds and
fish and snakes do what they want them to do.
JAMES 3:7

107

"Follow My teachings and learn from Me.
I am gentle and do not have pride. You will
have rest for your souls."
MATTHEW 11:29

108

But you, man of God, turn away from all
these sinful things. Work at being right with
God. Live a God-like life. Have faith and love.
Be willing to wait. Have a kind heart.
1 TIMOTHY 6:11

109

Your beauty should come from the inside. It
should come from the heart. This is the kind
that lasts. Your beauty should be a gentle and
quiet spirit. In God's sight this is of great worth
and no amount of money can buy it.
1 PETER 3:4

110

If the Holy Spirit is living in us,
let us be led by Him in all things.
GALATIANS 5:25

God Knows

Does it seem strange that God knows what you're going to do before you do it? He even knows what you're going to say before you say it. Crazy, right? . . . But it's true! God is omniscient. That means He knows absolutely everything. And because He knows you best (and loves you most), you can trust Him with everything. He already sees and knows what you're going through, and best of all. . .He cares. What an amazing promise!

111

Great is our Lord, and great in power.
His understanding has no end.
PSALM 147:5

112

Our heart may say that we have done wrong.
But remember, God is greater than our
heart. He knows everything.
1 JOHN 3:20

113

"Before I started to put you together in your mother, I knew you. Before you were born, I set you apart as holy. I chose you to speak to the nations for Me."

JEREMIAH 1:5

114

The eyes of the Lord are in every place, watching the bad and the good.

PROVERBS 15:3

115

Have you not known? Have you not heard? The God Who lives forever is the Lord, the One Who made the ends of the earth. He will not become weak or tired. His understanding is too great for us to begin to know.

ISAIAH 40:28

116

"Can a man hide himself in secret places so that I cannot see him?" says the Lord. "Do I not fill heaven and earth?" says the Lord.
JEREMIAH 23:24

117

He knows the number of the stars. He gives names to all of them. Great is our Lord, and great in power. His understanding has no end.
PSALM 147:4–5

118

*Even before I speak a word,
O Lord, You know it all.*
PSALM 139:4

119

"When you pray, do not say the same thing over and over again making long prayers like the people who do not know God. They think they are heard because their prayers are long. Do not be like them. Your Father knows what you need before you ask Him."

MATTHEW 6:7–8

120

"Are not two small birds sold for a very small piece of money? And yet not one of the birds falls to the earth without your Father knowing it."

MATTHEW 10:29

God's Assignments

God has great plans for you, courageous girl. Maybe you wonder, "What plans? He hasn't shown me anything!" That's one of the coolest things about God—He loves surprises. And He surely has some fantastic surprises in mind for you. As you get older, you're going to meet people, go places, and do things you never dreamed. He's got assignments (special plans for a special purpose) for you. Begin to pray now. Speak these words: "Lord, have Your way! Use me, I pray! Amen."

121

" 'For I know the plans I have for you,' says the Lord,
'plans for well-being and not for trouble,
to give you a future and a hope.' "

JEREMIAH 29:11

122

The mind of a man plans his way,
but the Lord shows him what to do.

PROVERBS 16:9

123

There are many plans in a man's heart,
but it is the Lord's plan that will stand.

PROVERBS 19:21

124

"Before I started to put you together in
your mother, I knew you. Before you were
born, I set you apart as holy. I chose you to
speak to the nations for Me."

JEREMIAH 1:5

125

*We know that God makes all things work
together for the good of those who love Him
and are chosen to be a part of His plan.*
ROMANS 8:28

126

*Trust in the Lord with all your heart,
and do not trust in your own understanding.
Agree with Him in all your ways,
and He will make your paths straight.*
PROVERBS 3:5–6

127

*"I know that You can do all things.
Nothing can put a stop to Your plans."*
JOB 42:2

128

I will show you and teach you in the way you should go. I will tell you what to do with My eye upon you.

PSALM 32:8

129

I am sure that God Who began the good work in you will keep on working in you until the day Jesus Christ comes again.

PHILIPPIANS 1:6

130

He is working in you. God is helping you obey Him. God is doing what He wants done in you.

PHILIPPIANS 2:13

God's Heart for the Lost

The Bible calls those who don't yet know Jesus "lost." But that's only because they don't know Him yet. Here's the good news: with your help, they can come to know Him. So, how does God feel about "lost" people? Does He only love believers? The truth is, the Lord adores all His kids, lost and saved! In fact, He's patiently waiting for the lost to fall in love with Him, because He already adores them. What a loving God we serve!

131

The Lord is not slow about keeping His promise as some people think. He is waiting for you. The Lord does not want any person to be punished forever. He wants all people to be sorry for their sins and turn from them.

2 PETER 3:9

132

For by His loving-favor you have been saved from the punishment of sin through faith. It is not by anything you have done. It is a gift of God. It is not given to you because you worked for it. If you could work for it, you would be proud.
EPHESIANS 2:8–9

133

"I tell you, there will be more joy in heaven because of one sinner who is sorry for his sins and turns from them, than for ninety-nine people right with God who do not have sins to be sorry for."
LUKE 15:7

134

"What if a woman has ten silver pieces of money and loses one of them? Does she not light a lamp and sweep the floor and look until she finds it? When she finds it, she calls her friends and neighbors together. She says to them, 'Be happy with me. I have found the piece of money I had lost.' I tell you, it is the same way among the angels of God. If one sinner is sorry for his sins and turns from them, the angels are very happy."

LUKE 15:8–10

135

"I am the Good Shepherd. The Good Shepherd gives His life for the sheep."

JOHN 10:11

136

Jesus sent out these twelve followers. He told them to go, saying, "Stay away from people who are not Jews. And do not go to any town in the country of Samaria. But go to the Jewish people who are lost."

MATTHEW 10:5–6

137

"For God so loved the world that He gave His only Son. Whoever puts his trust in God's Son will not be lost but will have life that lasts forever."
JOHN 3:16

138

You were like lost sheep. But now you have come back to Him Who is your Shepherd and the One Who cares for your soul.
1 PETER 2:25

139

"For the Son of Man came to look for and to save from the punishment of sin those who are lost."
LUKE 19:10

140

For the Lord God says, "I Myself will look for My sheep and find them."
EZEKIEL 34:11

God's Love

God adores you. . .it's true! His love for you is deeper than the deepest ocean, wider than the widest desert, and higher than the highest mountain. And there's nothing you can do to change that. What a remarkable promise! If you ever start to wonder, "Does God really love me, or does the Bible just say that?" you will find the answer here: He loves you so much that He sent His Son, Jesus, to die for your sins. Wow! Talk about amazing love!

141

"For God so loved the world that He gave His only Son. Whoever puts his trust in God's Son will not be lost but will have life that lasts forever."
JOHN 3:16

142

*The Lord your God is with you, a Powerful
One Who wins the battle. He will have much joy
over you. With His love He will give you new life.
He will have joy over you with loud singing.*

Zephaniah 3:17

143

*See what great love the Father has for us that He
would call us His children. And that is what we are.
For this reason the people of the world do not know
who we are because they did not know Him.*

1 John 3:1

144

*For I know that nothing can keep us from the
love of God. Death cannot! Life cannot! Angels
cannot! Leaders cannot! Any other power cannot!
Hard things now or in the future cannot!*

Romans 8:38

145

I have been put up on the cross to die with Christ. I no longer live. Christ lives in me. The life I now live in this body, I live by putting my trust in the Son of God. He was the One Who loved me and gave Himself for me.

GALATIANS 2:20

146

We love Him because He loved us first.

1 JOHN 4:19

147

But You, O Lord, are a God full of love and pity. You are slow to anger and rich in loving-kindness and truth.

PSALM 86:15

148

*The Lord came to us from far away,
saying, "I have loved you with a love that
lasts forever. So I have helped you come
to Me with loving-kindness."*
JEREMIAH 31:3

149

*Give thanks to the God of heaven,
for His loving-kindness lasts forever.*
PSALM 136:26

150

*My lips will praise You because Your
loving-kindness is better than life.*
PSALM 63:3

God's Way

You can't always figure out what God's up to, can you? Many times, things happen that seem unfair or confusing. But the Bible promises that the Lord is always ready to turn something bad into something good. (As some people like to say, He can turn a test into a testimony!) So, hang on during the tough times and remember this: His ways are higher than yours. And He loves you—which means He's looking out for you, even when bad things happen.

151

"For My thoughts are not your thoughts, and My ways are not your ways," says the Lord. "For as the heavens are higher than the earth, so are My ways higher than your ways, and My thoughts than your thoughts."
ISAIAH 55:8–9

152

Teach me Your way, O Lord.
I will walk in Your truth.
May my heart fear Your name.

PSALM 86:11

153

God's riches are so great! The things He
knows and His wisdom are so deep! No one
can understand His thoughts. No one can
understand His ways.

ROMANS 11:33

154

There is a way which looks right to a man,
but its end is the way of death.

PROVERBS 14:12

155

Many people will come and say, "Come, let us go up to the mountain of the Lord, to the house of the God of Jacob. Then He will teach us about His ways, that we may walk in His paths. For the Law will go out from Zion, and the Word of the Lord from Jerusalem."

Isaiah 2:3

156

Whoever is wise, let him understand these things and know them. For the ways of the Lord are right, and those who are right and good will follow them, but sinners will not follow them.

Hosea 14:9

157

He leads those without pride into what is right, and teaches them His way.

Psalm 25:9

158

Show me Your ways, O Lord.
Teach me Your paths.
PSALM 25:4

159

O Lord, I know that a man's way is not known by
himself. It is not in man to lead his own steps.
JEREMIAH 10:23

160

Trust in the Lord with all your heart,
and do not trust in your own understanding.
PROVERBS 3:5

Good Fruit

~~~~~~~~~~~~

Imagine you were an orange tree. The farmer took great care of you—provided everything you needed to produce great fruit during harvest season—but when the time came, you decided you didn't want any oranges growing on you. So you said, "Nah, I'm good!" God wants you to produce good fruit, just like a healthy orange tree. And He's given you everything you need to do good things and to show the world you're His child. Thank Him for that today!

161

But the fruit that comes from having the Holy Spirit in our lives is: love, joy, peace, not giving up, being kind, being good, having faith, being gentle, and being the boss over our own desires. The Law is not against these things.
GALATIANS 5:22–23

162

*"You have not chosen Me, I have chosen you.
I have set you apart for the work of bringing in
fruit. Your fruit should last. And whatever you ask
the Father in My name, He will give it to you."*

JOHN 15:16

163

*But the wisdom that comes from heaven is
first of all pure. Then it gives peace. It is gentle
and willing to obey. It is full of loving-kindness
and of doing good. It has no doubts and does
not pretend to be something it is not.*

JAMES 3:17

164

*"The heart is fooled more than anything else, and is
very sinful. Who can know how bad it is? I the Lord
look into the heart, and test the mind. I give to each
man what he should have because of his ways and
because of the fruit that comes from his works."*

JEREMIAH 17:9–10

165

"So you will know them by their fruit. Not everyone who says to me, 'Lord, Lord,' will go into the holy nation of heaven. The one who does the things My Father in heaven wants him to do will go into the holy nation of heaven."

MATTHEW 7:20–21

166

We are His work. He has made us to belong to Christ Jesus so we can work for Him. He planned that we should do this.

EPHESIANS 2:10

167

Then your lives will please the Lord. You will do every kind of good work, and you will know more about God.

COLOSSIANS 1:10

168

My Christian brothers, what good does it do if you say you have faith but do not do things that prove you have faith? Can that kind of faith save you from the punishment of sin? What if a Christian does not have clothes or food? And one of you says to him, "Goodbye, keep yourself warm and eat well." But if you do not give him what he needs, how does that help him?

JAMES 2:14–16

169

It is true, every good tree has good fruit. Every bad tree has bad fruit.

MATTHEW 7:17

170

Learn to do good. Look for what is right and fair. Speak strong words to those who make it hard for people. Stand up for the rights of those who have no parents. Help the woman whose husband has died.

ISAIAH 1:17

Gratitude

God loves it when you come to Him with a heart of gratitude. It brings Him great joy to know that you're thankful for all He's given you—your family, your home, your friends, even that pesky sibling! Remember, all good gifts come from the Lord. You don't deserve any of it; but in His Word He promises to lavish (pour) it out on you, simply because He adores you. So, show Him how grateful you are, courageous girl! Today. . .give thanks!

171

In everything give thanks. This is what God wants you to do because of Christ Jesus.
1 THESSALONIANS 5:18

172

Whatever you say or do, do it in the name of the Lord Jesus. Give thanks to God the Father through the Lord Jesus.
COLOSSIANS 3:17

173

Give thanks to the Lord, for He is good, for His loving-kindness lasts forever.
PSALM 136:1

174

Since then, I always give thanks for you and pray for you.
EPHESIANS 1:16

175

Let the peace of Christ have power over your hearts. You were chosen as a part of His body. Always be thankful.

COLOSSIANS 3:15

176

Since we have received a holy nation that cannot be moved, let us be thankful. Let us please God and worship Him with honor and fear.

HEBREWS 12:28

177

Give thanks to the Lord for He is good! His loving-kindness lasts forever!

PSALM 107:1

178

*"He who gives a gift of thanks honors Me.
And to him who makes his way right, I will
show him the saving power of God."*
PSALM 50:23

179

*You are my God and I will give You thanks.
You are my God and I will praise You.
Give thanks to the Lord, for He is good.
His loving-kindness lasts forever.*
PSALM 118:28–29

180

*Let us give thanks all the time to God through
Jesus Christ. Our gift to Him is to give thanks.
Our lips should always give thanks to His name.*
HEBREWS 13:15

Hard Work

Would you call yourself a hard worker? Sure, you do your schoolwork (and even tackle your homework), but do you always follow through when Mom says things like, "Get in there and clean your room, kiddo!" Maybe not. God loves it when His girls do the work—even the hard work. Sweeping the garage floor or cleaning up your baby brother's toys might not sound like fun, but when you do those things, you're proving to God that you're obedient. So, get to it, girl! You've got work to do!

181

Whatever work you do, do it with all your heart. Do it for the Lord and not for men.
COLOSSIANS 3:23

182

Some good comes from all work.
Nothing but talk leads only to being poor.
PROVERBS 14:23

183

Trust your work to the Lord, and your plans
will work out well.
PROVERBS 16:3

184

So if you eat or drink or whatever you do,
do everything to honor God.
1 CORINTHIANS 10:31

185

Do your best to live a quiet life. Learn to do your own work well. We told you about this before. By doing this, you will be respected by those who are not Christians. Then you will not be in need and others will not have to help you.

1 Thessalonians 4:11–12

186

Do not let yourselves get tired of doing good. If we do not give up, we will get what is coming to us at the right time.

Galatians 6:9

187

He who works his land will have all the bread he needs, but he who follows what is of no worth has no wisdom.

Proverbs 12:11

188

Let the favor of the Lord our God be upon us.
And make the work of our hands stand strong.
Yes, make the work of our hands stand strong.
PSALM 90:17

189

Do you see a man who is good at his work?
He will stand in front of kings. He will not stand
in front of men who are not important.
PROVERBS 22:29

190

The Lord will finish the work He started for me.
O Lord, Your loving-kindness lasts forever.
Do not turn away from the works of Your hands.
PSALM 138:8

Health

If you read the Bible, you know that Jesus went from place to place, healing the sick. He never turned anyone away, no matter who they were or what they'd done. Here's a fun fact: God is still in the healing business. It's true! You'll find that promise in His Word. He can heal diseases, but He can also heal broken hearts and fix broken relationships. If you're in need of healing, go to Him and ask. He's excited to hear from you and wants to give you a healthy life.

191

Dear friend, I pray that you are doing well in every way. I pray that your body is strong and well even as your soul is.
3 John 1:2

192

A glad heart is good medicine,
but a broken spirit dries up the bones.
PROVERBS 17:22

193

He said, "Listen well to the voice of the Lord
your God. Do what is right in His eyes. Listen to
what He tells you, and obey all His Laws. If you
do this, I will put none of the diseases on you
which I have put on the Egyptians. For I am
the Lord Who heals you."
EXODUS 15:26

194

Do not be wise in your own eyes. Fear the Lord and turn away from what is sinful. It will be healing to your body and medicine to your bones.
PROVERBS 3:7–8

195

Pleasing words are like honey. They are sweet to the soul and healing to the bones.
PROVERBS 16:24

196

Serve the Lord your God and He will give you bread and water. And I will take sickness from among you.
EXODUS 23:25

197

He heals those who have a broken heart. He heals their sorrows.
PSALM 147:3

198

"For I will heal you. I will heal you where you have been hurt," says the Lord, "because they have said that you are not wanted. They have said, 'It is Zion. No one cares for her.'"

JEREMIAH 30:17

199

*But He was hurt for our wrong-doing.
He was crushed for our sins. He was
punished so we would have peace.
He was beaten so we would be healed.*

ISAIAH 53:5

200

He carried our sins in His own body when He died on a cross. In doing this, we may be dead to sin and alive to all that is right and good. His wounds have healed you!

1 PETER 2:24

Helping Those in Need

This big, wide world is filled with people in need. Some need food. Some need clothes and shoes. Here's the cool thing: you can be the hands and feet of Jesus by helping those in need. You can donate food to your church's food pantry, donate clothes you've outgrown, and even work (with your parents) at a homeless shelter. No matter how you decide to help, do so with a smile on your face and the love of Jesus in your heart. He promises to bless you as you bless others.

201

"For I was hungry and you gave Me food to eat. I was thirsty and you gave Me water to drink. I was a stranger and you gave Me a room. I had no clothes and you gave Me clothes to wear. I was sick and you cared for Me. I was in prison and you came to see Me."
MATTHEW 25:35–36

202

*If you see your brother's donkey or his ox
fallen down by the road, do not pretend
that you do not see them. Be sure to help
him lift them up again.*

DEUTERONOMY 22:4

203

*Help each other in troubles and problems.
This is the kind of law Christ asks us to obey.*

GALATIANS 6:2

204

*He who gives much will be honored,
for he gives some of his food to the poor.*

PROVERBS 22:9

205

"In every way I showed you that by working hard like this we can help those who are weak. We must remember what the Lord Jesus said, 'We are more happy when we give than when we receive.'"
ACTS 20:35

206

The poor will always be in the land. So I tell you to be free in giving to your brother, to those in need, and to the poor in your land.
DEUTERONOMY 15:11

207

He who shows kindness to a poor man gives to the Lord and He will pay him in return for his good act.
PROVERBS 19:17

208

"Sell what you have and give the money to poor people. Have money-bags for yourselves that will never wear out. These money-bags are riches in heaven that will always be there. No robber can take them and no bugs can eat them there."
LUKE 12:33

209

What if a person has enough money to live on and sees his brother in need of food and clothing? If he does not help him, how can the love of God be in him?
1 JOHN 3:17

210

He who makes it hard for the poor brings shame to his Maker, but he who shows loving-favor to those in need honors Him.
PROVERBS 14:31

Jesus Loves Me

"Jesus loves me, this I know". . . These words are so much more than a child's song—they are truth that will guide you and give you joy, peace, and strength for all your life. And it's a biblical promise! Nothing you can ever do will stop Jesus from loving you. He adores you—on good days and bad. So, why not share that love with others today!

211

For God so loved the world that He gave His only Son. Whoever puts his trust in God's Son will not be lost but will have life that lasts forever.
JOHN 3:16

212

*But God had so much loving-kindness. He loved
us with such a great love. Even when we were
dead because of our sins, He made us alive by
what Christ did for us. You have been saved from
the punishment of sin by His loving-favor.*
EPHESIANS 2:4–5

213

*But God showed His love to us.
While we were still sinners, Christ died for us.*
ROMANS 5:8

214

*The Lord your God is with you, a Powerful One
Who wins the battle. He will have much joy over
you. With His love He will give you new life.
He will have joy over you with loud singing.*
ZEPHANIAH 3:17

215

We have come to know and believe the love God has for us. God is love. If you live in love, you live by the help of God and God lives in you.
1 JOHN 4:16

216

See what great love the Father has for us that He would call us His children. And that is what we are. For this reason the people of the world do not know who we are because they did not know Him.
1 JOHN 3:1

217

We love Him because He loved us first.
1 JOHN 4:19

218

*But You, O Lord, are a God full of love
and pity. You are slow to anger and rich
in loving-kindness and truth.*
PSALM 86:15

219

*The Lord came to us from far away,
saying, "I have loved you with a love that
lasts forever. So I have helped you come
to Me with loving-kindness."*
JEREMIAH 31:3

220

*"No one can have greater love than
to give his life for his friends."*
JOHN 15:13

Joy Is Yours!

Are you a happy girl? Would people describe you as joyful and filled with life? That's good! God wants His girls to overflow with joy. Of course, life isn't always easy. You will sometimes have struggles. There will still be pain and heartache from time to time. But even in the middle of all of that, if your heart is filled with the kind of joy that only Jesus can bring, He promises to bring you through with a smile on your face.

221

Our hope comes from God. May He fill you with joy and peace because of your trust in Him. May your hope grow stronger by the power of the Holy Spirit.
ROMANS 15:13

222

*Be full of joy always because you belong to
the Lord. Again I say, be full of joy!*
PHILIPPIANS 4:4

223

*My Christian brothers, you should be happy
when you have all kinds of tests.*
JAMES 1:2

224

*"Until now you have not asked for
anything in My name. Ask and you will
receive. Then your joy will be full."*
JOHN 16:24

225

A glad heart is good medicine,
but a broken spirit dries up the bones.
PROVERBS 17:22

226

You will show me the way of life. Being
with You is to be full of joy. In Your right
hand there is happiness forever.
PSALM 16:11

227

This is the day that the Lord has made.
Let us be full of joy and be glad in it.
PSALM 118:24

228

*"I have told you these things so My joy
may be in you and your joy may be full."*
JOHN 15:11

229

*For His anger lasts only a short time. But His
favor is for life. Crying may last for a night,
but joy comes with the new day.*
PSALM 30:5

230

*My Christian brothers, you should be happy
when you have all kinds of tests. You know
these prove your faith. It helps you not to give
up. Learn well how to wait so you will be strong
and complete and in need of nothing.*
JAMES 1:2–4

Kindness

Do you show kindness to others? Maybe you have to pause and think about that. Some people are easier to treat with kindness, after all. But God wants you to be kind to everyone. That girl who's mean to you? Respond with kindness. That little brother who annoys you? Him too. It might seem impossible, but as you practice kindness, you'll get better at it. And guess what? It's contagious! So, let your kindness show, courageous girl!

231

You must be kind to each other. Think of the other person. Forgive other people just as God forgave you because of Christ's death on the cross.
EPHESIANS 4:32

232

The man who shows loving-kindness does himself good, but the man without pity hurts himself.
PROVERBS 11:17

233

God has chosen you. You are holy and loved by Him. Because of this, your new life should be full of loving-pity. You should be kind to others and have no pride. Be gentle and be willing to wait for others.
COLOSSIANS 3:12

234

She opens her mouth with wisdom. The teaching of kindness is on her tongue.
PROVERBS 31:26

235

Love does not give up. Love is kind. Love is not jealous. Love does not put itself up as being important. Love has no pride. Love does not do the wrong thing. Love never thinks of itself. Love does not get angry. Love does not remember the suffering that comes from being hurt by someone.
1 Corinthians 13:4–5

236

Because of this, we should do good to everyone. For sure, we should do good to those who belong to Christ.
Galatians 6:10

237

But the fruit that comes from having the Holy Spirit in our lives is: love, joy, peace, not giving up, being kind, being good, having faith.
Galatians 5:22

238

*We see how kind God is. It shows how hard
He is also. He is hard on those who fall away.
But He is kind to you if you keep on trusting
Him. If you do not, He will cut you off.*
ROMANS 11:22

239

*O man, He has told you what is good. What does
the Lord ask of you but to do what is fair and to love
kindness, and to walk without pride with your God?*
MICAH 6:8

240

*He who follows what is right and loving and kind
finds life, right-standing with God and honor.*
PROVERBS 21:21

Light in the Darkness

Have you ever been in a very dark room—where you couldn't see a thing? It's kind of scary, isn't it? People across this world are walking in darkness, and they don't even realize it. They haven't seen the light of Jesus yet. Will you let Him shine through you, so that others can see and come to know Him? He promises to use you if you ask. It's the greatest thing in the world to lead others to their Savior by letting your light shine!

241

Jesus spoke to all the people, saying, "I am the Light of the world. Anyone who follows Me will not walk in darkness. He will have the Light of Life."
JOHN 8:12

242

The Light shines in the darkness. The darkness has never been able to put out the Light.
JOHN 1:5

243

*Your Word is a lamp to my feet
and a light to my path.*
PSALM 119:105

244

*"Let your light shine in front of men. Then
they will see the good things you do and will
honor your Father Who is in heaven."*
MATTHEW 5:16

245

*If we live in the light as He is in the light,
we share what we have in God with each
other. And the blood of Jesus Christ, His Son,
makes our lives clean from all sin.*
1 JOHN 1:7

246

*At one time you lived in darkness. Now
you are living in the light that comes
from the Lord. Live as children who have
the light of the Lord in them.*
EPHESIANS 5:8

247

"You are the light of the world. You cannot hide a city that is on a mountain."
MATTHEW 5:14

248

But you are a chosen group of people. You are the King's religious leaders. You are a holy nation. You belong to God. He has done this for you so you can tell others how God has called you out of darkness into His great light.
1 PETER 2:9

249

This is what we heard Him tell us. We are passing it on to you. God is light. There is no darkness in Him.
1 JOHN 1:5

250

The Lord is my light and the One Who saves me. Whom should I fear? The Lord is the strength of my life. Of whom should I be afraid?
PSALM 27:1

Love's Promise

What is love, exactly? God's Word has a lot to say on the subject! Love is more than just a feeling; it's a dedication that puts the needs of others above your own. God loved us first. And because He showed us how to love, we can know how to love others well— even the people who are difficult to love. You're a precious girl, and God is so proud of the way you love others!

251

I may be able to speak the languages of men and even of angels, but if I do not have love, it will sound like noisy brass. If I have the gift of speaking God's Word and if I understand all secrets, but do not have love, I am nothing. If I know all things and if I have the gift of faith so I can move mountains, but do not have love, I am nothing.
1 CORINTHIANS 13:1–2

252

Love does not give up. Love is kind. Love is not jealous. Love does not put itself up as being important. Love has no pride.
1 CORINTHIANS 13:4

253

Love does not do the wrong thing. Love never thinks of itself. Love does not get angry. Love does not remember the suffering that comes from being hurt by someone.

1 CORINTHIANS 13:5

254

Love is not happy with sin. Love is happy with the truth. Love takes everything that comes without giving up. Love believes all things. Love hopes for all things. Love keeps on in all things.

1 CORINTHIANS 13:6–7

255

And now we have these three: faith and hope and love, but the greatest of these is love.

1 CORINTHIANS 13:13

256

For God so loved the world that He gave His only Son. Whoever puts his trust in God's Son will not be lost but will have life that lasts forever.

JOHN 3:16

257

*Those who do not love do not know
God because God is love.*
1 John 4:8

258

*Most of all, have a true love for each other.
Love covers many sins.*
1 Peter 4:8

259

*"I give you a new Law. You are to love each
other. You must love each other as I have
loved you. If you love each other, all men will
know you are My followers."*
John 13:34–35

260

We love Him because He loved us first.
1 John 4:19

Make Each Day Count

How do you spend your days? Do you play? Do schoolwork? Eat meals with your family? Clean your room? Sleep? Start all over again the next day? God wants you to be wise about how you spend your time. In the middle of your busyness, don't forget to make time for Him. God promises that if you pray and read your Bible, you will grow in your faith. . .so make every day count!

261

Teach us to understand how many days we have.
Then we will have a heart of wisdom to give You.
PSALM 90:12

262

So be careful how you live. Live as men who are
wise and not foolish. Make the best use of your
time. These are sinful days. Do not be foolish.
Understand what the Lord wants you to do.
EPHESIANS 5:15–17

263

Be wise in the way you live around those who are not Christians. Make good use of your time.
COLOSSIANS 4:5

264

We do not look at the things that can be seen. We look at the things that cannot be seen. The things that can be seen will come to an end. But the things that cannot be seen will last forever.
2 CORINTHIANS 4:18

265

He has made everything beautiful in its time. He has put thoughts of the forever in man's mind, yet man cannot understand the work God has done from the beginning to the end.
ECCLESIASTES 3:11

266

We are sure of this. We know that while we are at home in this body we are not with the Lord. Our life is lived by faith. We do not live by what we see in front of us.
2 CORINTHIANS 5:6–7

267

*Do not talk much about tomorrow,
for you do not know what a day will bring.*
PROVERBS 27:1

268

*Listen! You who say, "Today or tomorrow we will
go to this city and stay a year and make money."
You do not know about tomorrow. What is your
life? It is like fog. You see it and soon it is gone.*
JAMES 4:13–14

269

*The mind of a man plans his way,
but the Lord shows him what to do.*
PROVERBS 16:9

270

*As for me, I will call on God and the Lord
will save me. I will cry out and complain
in the evening and morning and noon,
and He will hear my voice.*
PSALM 55:16–17

Me, Myself, and I?

"I want what I want, and I want it now!" Have you ever been guilty of using (or thinking) those words? Most human beings are a little selfish. It's hard not to put your own needs first. But God wants you to let go of that "me, myself, and I" attitude and begin to love others as you love yourself. This can only happen if you love Him most of all. When you do, He promises to show you how to best love and serve others.

271

What if a person has enough money to live on and sees his brother in need of food and clothing? If he does not help him, how can the love of God be in him?
1 John 3:17

272

Love does not do the wrong thing. Love never thinks of itself. Love does not get angry. Love does not remember the suffering that comes from being hurt by someone.
1 Corinthians 13:5

273

Nothing should be done because of pride or thinking about yourself. Think of other people as more important than yourself. Do not always be thinking about your own plans only. Be happy to know what other people are doing.
PHILIPPIANS 2:3–4

274

Do not work only for your own good. Think of what you can do for others.
1 CORINTHIANS 10:24

275

Help each other in troubles and problems. This is the kind of law Christ asks us to obey.
GALATIANS 6:2

276

We who have strong faith should help those who are weak. We should not live to please ourselves. Each of us should live to please his neighbor. This will help him grow in faith. Even Christ did not please Himself. The Holy Writings say, "The sharp words spoken against you fell on Me."
ROMANS 15:1–3

277

*Remember to do good and help each other.
Gifts like this please God.*
HEBREWS 13:16

278

*Those who love only themselves and do not
obey the truth, but do what is wrong, will be
punished by God. His anger will be on them.*
ROMANS 2:8

279

*Then Jesus said to them all, "If anyone wants
to follow Me, he must give up himself and
his own desires. He must take up his cross
everyday and follow Me."*
LUKE 9:23

280

*What if a Christian does not have clothes or food?
And one of you says to him, "Goodbye, keep
yourself warm and eat well." But if you do not give
him what he needs, how does that help him? A faith
that does not do things is a dead faith.*
JAMES 2:15–17

Neighbors

"Who is my neighbor?" one man asked Jesus. Our Savior responded by telling him a story about a guy who cared for a stranger who had been injured. According to God, everyone is our neighbor! So, when He says, "Love your neighbor," He's not just talking about the family next door. Jesus wants you to treat all the people you meet just as you would treat your next-door neighbor—with love, kindness, and generosity.

281

"The second Law is this: 'You must love your neighbor as yourself.' No other Law is greater than these."
MARK 12:31

282

You do well when you obey the Holy Writings which say, "You must love your neighbor as you love yourself."
JAMES 2:8

283

Each of us should live to please his neighbor.
This will help him grow in faith.
ROMANS 15:2

284

You obey the whole Law when you do this one thing,
"Love your neighbor as you love yourself."
GALATIANS 5:14

285

Do not plan for your neighbor to be hurt,
while he trusts you enough to live beside you.
PROVERBS 3:29

286

The man said, "You must love the Lord your God
with all your heart. You must love Him with all your
soul. You must love Him with all your strength. You
must love Him with all your mind. You must love
your neighbor as you love yourself."
LUKE 10:27

287

Anyone who loves his neighbor will do no wrong to him. You keep the Law with love.
ROMANS 13:10

288

"Do for other people what you would like to have them do for you."
LUKE 6:31

289

Because of this, we should do good to everyone. For sure, we should do good to those who belong to Christ.
GALATIANS 6:10

290

"Do not tell a lie about your neighbor."
EXODUS 20:16

Offense

"I'm so offended!" Have you ever used those words? It's easy to get your feelings hurt when people say mean things or leave you out. But God doesn't want you to be offended. He wants you to forgive the person who hurt you and move on. When you live like this, He promises to give you peace in your heart. You'll also build lasting friendships while you're shining the light of Jesus for all to see.

291

A man's understanding makes him slow to anger. It is to his honor to forgive and forget a wrong done to him.
PROVERBS 19:11

292

A brother who has been hurt in his spirit is harder to be won than a strong city, and arguing is like the iron gates of a king's house.
PROVERBS 18:19

293

"Watch yourselves! If your brother sins, speak sharp words to him. If he is sorry and turns from his sin, forgive him. What if he sins against you seven times in one day? If he comes to you and says he is sorry and turns from his sin, forgive him."
LUKE 17:3–4

294

Live and work without pride. Be gentle and kind. Do not be hard on others. Let love keep you from doing that. Work hard to live together as one by the help of the Holy Spirit. Then there will be peace.
EPHESIANS 4:2–3

295

My Christian brothers, you know everyone should listen much and speak little. He should be slow to become angry.

JAMES 1:19

296

A servant owned by God must not make trouble. He must be kind to everyone. He must be able to teach. He must be willing to suffer when hurt for doing good.

2 TIMOTHY 2:24

297

"You are happy when men hate you and do not want you around and put shame on you because you trust in Me. Be glad in that day. Be full of joy for your reward is much in heaven. Their fathers did these things to the early preachers."

LUKE 6:22–23

298

The anger of a fool is known at once, but a wise man does not speak when he is spoken against.
PROVERBS 12:16

299

If men speak bad of you because you are a Christian, you will be happy because the Spirit of shining-greatness and of God is in you.
1 PETER 4:14

300

Whoever hits you on one side of the face, turn so he can hit the other side also. Whoever takes your coat, give him your shirt also.
LUKE 6:29

Offering

God is a giver. He gave His Son, Jesus, who gave His life. The Holy Spirit gives peace and comfort. God just keeps on giving and giving and giving some more. And He wants you to be a giver too. He wants you to offer your heart, your money, your talents, and your abilities. Most of all, He wants you to offer your life in service to Him. When you do, He will take you places you never dreamed you would go! What a precious promise!

301

Each man should give as he has decided in his heart. He should not give, wishing he could keep it. Or he should not give if he feels he has to give. God loves a man who gives because he wants to give.

2 CORINTHIANS 9:7

302

"Give, and it will be given to you. You will have more than enough. It can be pushed down and shaken together and it will still run over as it is given to you. The way you give to others is the way you will receive in return."

LUKE 6:38

303

"Do not worry. Do not keep saying, 'What will we eat?' or, 'What will we drink?' or, 'What will we wear?' The people who do not know God are looking for all these things. Your Father in heaven knows you need all these things. First of all, look for the holy nation of God. Be right with Him. All these other things will be given to you also."

MATTHEW 6:31–33

304

*Every man should give as he is able,
as the Lord your God has given to you.*
DEUTERONOMY 16:17

305

*Let us give thanks all the time to God through
Jesus Christ. Our gift to Him is to give thanks.
Our lips should always give thanks to His name.*
HEBREWS 13:15

306

*Christian brothers, I ask you from my heart
to give your bodies to God because of His
loving-kindness to us. Let your bodies be
a living and holy gift given to God. He is
pleased with this kind of gift. This is the true
worship that you should give Him.*
ROMANS 12:1

307

*For wherever your riches are,
your heart will be there also.*
Matthew 6:21

308

*For God so loved the world that He gave His only
Son. Whoever puts his trust in God's Son will not
be lost but will have life that lasts forever.*
John 3:16

309

*Remember to do good and help each other.
Gifts like this please God.*
Hebrews 13:16

310

*There is one who is free in giving, and yet he
grows richer. And there is one who keeps what
he should give, but he ends up needing more.*
Proverbs 11:24

Overcoming

What does it mean to be an overcomer? Does it mean everything goes your way and you will win every battle? Not at all! If anyone knew what it was like to be an overcomer, it was Jesus. He's got the best battle record ever! To be like Him, you simply have to step out in faith, no matter what life throws your way. Every problem you face will be resolved in God's way and God's time if you just trust in Him. That's a promise you can take to the bank!

311

"I have told you these things so you may have peace in Me. In the world you will have much trouble. But take hope! I have power over the world!"
JOHN 16:33

312

*I can do all things because
Christ gives me the strength.*
Philippians 4:13

313

*Every child of God has power over the sins
of the world. The way we have power over
the sins of the world is by our faith. Who
could have power over the world except by
believing that Jesus is the Son of God?*
1 John 5:4–5

314

*I will allow the one who has power and
wins to sit with Me on My throne, as I
also had power and won and sat down
with My Father on His throne.*
Revelation 3:21

315

*He who has power and
wins will receive these things.
I will be his God and he will be My son.*
REVELATION 21:7

316

*But God is the One Who gives us power
over sin through Jesus Christ our Lord.
We give thanks to Him for this.*
1 CORINTHIANS 15:57

317

*But we have power over all these things
through Jesus Who loves us so much.*
ROMANS 8:37

318

The Lord is my strength and my safe cover. My heart trusts in Him, and I am helped. So my heart is full of joy. I will thank Him with my song.

PSALM 28:7

319

The Lord is my light and the One Who saves me. Whom should I fear? The Lord is the strength of my life. Of whom should I be afraid?

PSALM 27:1

320

Do not worry. Learn to pray about everything. Give thanks to God as you ask Him for what you need. The peace of God is much greater than the human mind can understand. This peace will keep your hearts and minds through Christ Jesus.

PHILIPPIANS 4:6–7

Patience

Want a burger? Drive through a fast-food restaurant. Need to eat quickly at home? Pop something in the microwave. These days no one wants to wait for anything. Maybe you're the same. You have a hard time waiting for Christmas. Or birthdays. Or for someone you love to do the right thing. God knows what it's like to wait. He waits a long time for some of His kids to do the right thing too. Be patient, courageous girl! God's Word promises that your patience will be rewarded if you don't give up.

321

*Be happy in your hope. Do not give up
when trouble comes. Do not let anything
stop you from praying.*
ROMANS 12:12

322

Do not let yourselves get tired of doing good. If we do not give up, we will get what is coming to us at the right time.

GALATIANS 6:9

323

But if we hope for something we do not yet see, we must learn how to wait for it.

ROMANS 8:25

324

Live and work without pride. Be gentle and kind. Do not be hard on others. Let love keep you from doing that.

EPHESIANS 4:2

325

Rest in the Lord and be willing to wait for Him. Do not trouble yourself when all goes well with the one who carries out his sinful plans.
PSALM 37:7

326

But they who wait upon the Lord will get new strength. They will rise up with wings like eagles. They will run and not get tired. They will walk and not become weak.
ISAIAH 40:31

327

The Lord is good to those who wait for Him, to the one who looks for Him.
LAMENTATIONS 3:25

328

I did not give up waiting for the Lord.
And He turned to me and heard my cry.
PSALM 40:1

329

You must be willing to wait also. Be strong in your
hearts because the Lord is coming again soon.
JAMES 5:8

330

Christian brothers, be willing to wait for the
Lord to come again. Learn from the farmer.
He waits for the good fruit from the earth
until the early and late rains come.
JAMES 5:7

Peace

God wants you to have peace in your heart. You might say, "Wow! Does He know what I'm going through? Peace feels impossible with all the stuff I'm facing." But peace is possible, even in the middle of life's storms. Troubles will come, yes. But if you walk closely with Jesus—if you don't take your eyes off Him—God promises to bless you with supernatural peace. So, keep your thoughts on Him, no matter what!

331

"I have told you these things so you may have peace in Me. In the world you will have much trouble. But take hope! I have power over the world!"

JOHN 16:33

332

*May the Lord of peace give you His peace
at all times. The Lord be with you all.*
2 THESSALONIANS 3:16

333

*You will keep the man in perfect peace whose
mind is kept on You, because he trusts in You.*
ISAIAH 26:3

334

*"Those who make peace are happy,
because they will be called the sons of God."*
MATTHEW 5:9

335

As much as you can,
live in peace with all men.
<small>ROMANS 12:18</small>

336

Let the peace of Christ have power over
your hearts. You were chosen as a part of
His body. Always be thankful.
<small>COLOSSIANS 3:15</small>

337

Be at peace with all men. Live a holy
life. No one will see the Lord without
having that kind of life.
<small>HEBREWS 12:14</small>

338

"Peace I leave with you. My peace I give to you.
I do not give peace to you as the world gives.
Do not let your hearts be troubled or afraid."

JOHN 14:27

339

I will lie down and sleep in peace.
O Lord, You alone keep me safe.

PSALM 4:8

340

Turn away from what is sinful.
Do what is good. Look for peace and go after it.

1 PETER 3:11

Prayer

What if talking to God could be as natural and comfortable as talking to a good friend? It should be! The Lord wants you to spend time telling Him all you're going through—the good and the bad. He wants to be the first person you run to when you're hurting, and the first person you tell your good news. And remember, prayer is not a one-way conversation. If you listen closely, God is speaking to your heart too!

341

Do not worry. Learn to pray about everything. Give thanks to God as you ask Him for what you need.
PHILIPPIANS 4:6

342

"Because of this, I say to you, whatever you ask for when you pray, have faith that you will receive it. Then you will get it."
MARK 11:24

343

Never stop praying.
1 THESSALONIANS 5:17

344

In the same way, the Holy Spirit helps us where we are weak. We do not know how to pray or what we should pray for, but the Holy Spirit prays to God for us with sounds that cannot be put into words.
ROMANS 8:26

345

"When you pray, go into a room by yourself.
After you have shut the door, pray to your
Father Who is in secret. Then your Father
Who sees in secret will reward you."
MATTHEW 6:6

346

Tell your sins to each other. And pray for each
other so you may be healed. The prayer from the
heart of a man right with God has much power.
JAMES 5:16

347

"Call to Me, and I will answer you. And I
will show you great and wonderful things
which you do not know."
JEREMIAH 33:3

348

"Pray like this: 'Our Father in heaven, Your name is holy. May Your holy nation come. What You want done, may it be done on earth as it is in heaven.' "

MATTHEW 6:9–10

349

Jesus told them a picture-story to show that men should always pray and not give up.

LUKE 18:1

350

I want men everywhere to pray. They should lift up holy hands as they pray. They should not be angry or argue.

1 TIMOTHY 2:8

Pride

Have you ever met someone who's prideful? Maybe she thinks she's the prettiest or the most talented. Maybe he thinks he's the smartest kid in school. God isn't a big fan of pride. In fact, His Word says that pride leads to a fall. (Watch out if you start bragging on yourself! You might just take a tumble!) Instead of singing your own praises, praise God and others. As you lift them up, God will lift you up! What a sweet promise!

351

*When pride comes, then comes shame,
but wisdom is with those who have no pride.*
PROVERBS 11:2

352

*Pride comes before being destroyed
and a proud spirit comes before a fall.*
PROVERBS 16:18

353

*A man's pride will bring him down, but he whose
spirit is without pride will receive honor.*
PROVERBS 29:23

354

*But He gives us more loving-favor. For the Holy
Writings say, "God works against the proud but
gives loving-favor to those who have no pride."*
JAMES 4:6

355

Do not love the world or anything in the world. If anyone loves the world, the Father's love is not in him. For everything that is in the world does not come from the Father. The desires of our flesh and the things our eyes see and want and the pride of this life come from the world.
1 JOHN 2:15–16

356

Live in peace with each other. Do not act or think with pride. Be happy to be with poor people. Keep yourself from thinking you are so wise.
ROMANS 12:16

357

If anyone thinks he is important when he is nothing, he is fooling himself.
GALATIANS 6:3

358

Nothing should be done because of pride or thinking about yourself. Think of other people as more important than yourself.
PHILIPPIANS 2:3

359

*Let another man praise you,
and not your own mouth.
Let a stranger, and not your own lips.*
PROVERBS 27:2

360

*Eyes lifted high and a proud heart is sin
and is the lamp of the sinful.*
PROVERBS 21:4

Problems

Have you ever wished you could live a problem-free life? Things would be much easier if you didn't have so many bumps in the road. But think about it like this: problems are great opportunities to learn life's lessons. If you never had problems, God wouldn't have to come up with solutions! He wants to prove that He's bigger than anything you might face, so don't panic when troubles come. He promises to give an answer!

361

Those who are right with the Lord cry,
and He hears them. And He takes them
from all their troubles.
PSALM 34:17

362

The man who does not give up when tests come is happy. After the test is over, he will receive the crown of life. God has promised this to those who love Him.
JAMES 1:12

363

"I have told you these things so you may have peace in Me. In the world you will have much trouble. But take hope! I have power over the world!"
JOHN 16:33

364

But the Lord knows how to help men who are right with God when they are tempted. He also knows how to keep the sinners suffering for their wrong-doing until the day they stand before God Who will judge them.
2 PETER 2:9

365

*He who watches over his mouth
and his tongue keeps his soul from troubles.*
PROVERBS 21:23

366

*The one who is right with God is kept from trouble,
but the sinful get into trouble instead.*
PROVERBS 11:8

367

*We know that God makes all things work
together for the good of those who love Him
and are chosen to be a part of His plan.*
ROMANS 8:28

368

Our hope comes from God. May He fill you with joy and peace because of your trust in Him. May your hope grow stronger by the power of the Holy Spirit.

ROMANS 15:13

369

After you have suffered for awhile, God Himself will make you perfect. He will keep you in the right way. He will give you strength. He is the God of all loving-favor and has called you through Christ Jesus to share His shining-greatness forever.

1 PETER 5:10

370

Do not fear, for I am with you. Do not be afraid, for I am your God. I will give you strength, and for sure I will help you. Yes, I will hold you up with My right hand that is right and good.

ISAIAH 41:10

Run the Race

Have you ever run a race? When you start, it seems like so much fun. You're absolutely sure you can make it all the way to the finish line. But, as you run, you start to get out of breath. Your legs feel funny. You get thirsty. You wonder if you'll make it to the end. Life is a lot like a race. God wants you to keep going—even when you don't feel like it. When you do what His Word says, He promises you'll take the prize at the end!

371

You know that only one person gets a crown for being in a race even if many people run. You must run so you will win the crown.
1 CORINTHIANS 9:24

372

All these many people who have had faith in God are around us like a cloud. Let us put every thing out of our lives that keeps us from doing what we should. Let us keep running in the race that God has planned for us.
HEBREWS 12:1

373

I have fought a good fight. I have finished the work I was to do. I have kept the faith.
2 TIMOTHY 4:7

374

No, Christian brothers, I do not have that life yet. But I do one thing. I forget everything that is behind me and look forward to that which is ahead of me. My eyes are on the crown. I want to win the race and get the crown of God's call from heaven through Christ Jesus.
PHILIPPIANS 3:13–14

375

You were doing well. Who stopped you from obeying the truth?
GALATIANS 5:7

376

"But the one who stays true to the end will be saved."
MATTHEW 24:13

377

Fight the good fight of faith. Take hold of the life that lasts forever. You were chosen to receive it. You have spoken well about this life in front of many people.
1 Timothy 6:12

378

I will run the way of Your Law, for You will give me a willing heart.
Psalm 119:32

379

You must be willing to wait without giving up. After you have done what God wants you to do, God will give you what He promised you.
Hebrews 10:36

380

Anyone who runs in a race must follow the rules to get the crown.
2 Timothy 2:5

School Days

From the day you're born, you're always learning. You learn how to eat, how to walk, and how to talk. As you get older and go to school, you learn all sorts of things—math, science, geography, and much more. You learn how to sit still and pay attention and how to treat adults with respect. God loves it that you're a willing learner. He's got so much more to teach you as life goes on. Will you be a happy student?

381

A wise man will hear and grow in learning.
A man of understanding will become able.
PROVERBS 1:5

382

The fear of the Lord is the beginning of much learning. Fools hate wisdom and teaching.
PROVERBS 1:7

383

*An understanding mind gets much learning,
and the ear of the wise listens for much learning.*
PROVERBS 18:15

384

*Give teaching to a wise man and he will be
even wiser. Teach a man who is right and good,
and he will grow in learning.*
PROVERBS 9:9

385

*Keep on doing all the things you learned
and received and heard from me. Do the
things you saw me do. Then the God Who
gives peace will be with you.*
PHILIPPIANS 4:9

386

You must teach what is right and true.
TITUS 2:1

387

All the Holy Writings are God-given and are made alive by Him. Man is helped when he is taught God's Word. It shows what is wrong. It changes the way of a man's life. It shows him how to be right with God.

2 Timothy 3:16

388

Jesus grew strong in mind and body. He grew in favor with God and men.

Luke 2:52

389

I will show you and teach you in the way you should go. I will tell you what to do with My eye upon you.

Psalm 32:8

390

"The Helper is the Holy Spirit. The Father will send Him in My place. He will teach you everything and help you remember everything I have told you."

John 14:26

Self-Control

Control yourself! Maybe you've heard your mom speak those words. Oh, but it's hard to control yourself, especially if you're upset. It's also hard when you're tempted to do the wrong thing—like eat the whole cake instead of just one slice. It takes a lot of self-control to say no to your own desires and wishes, but the Lord really wants you to do your very best, courageous girl. And don't worry! The Holy Spirit will help you, if you just ask. That's a promise!

391

A man who cannot rule his own spirit is like a city whose walls are broken down.
PROVERBS 25:28

392

But the fruit that comes from having the Holy Spirit in our lives is: love, joy, peace, not giving up, being kind, being good, having faith, being gentle, and being the boss over our own desires. The Law is not against these things.
GALATIANS 5:22–23

393

As you have a better understanding, be able to say no when you need to. Do not give up. And as you wait and do not give up, live God-like.
2 Peter 1:6

394

He who is slow to anger is better than the powerful. And he who rules his spirit is better than he who takes a city.
Proverbs 16:32

395

The end of the world is near. You must be the boss over your mind. Keep awake so you can pray.
1 Peter 4:7

396

He must like to take people into his home. He must love what is good. He must be able to think well and do all things in the right way. He must live a holy life and be the boss over his own desires.
Titus 1:8

397

We are taught to have nothing to do with that which is against God. We are to have nothing to do with the desires of this world. We are to be wise and to be right with God. We are to live God-like lives in this world.

TITUS 2:12

398

Older men are to be quiet and to be careful how they act. They are to be the boss over their own desires. Their faith and love are to stay strong and they are not to give up.

TITUS 2:2

399

A fool always loses his temper, but a wise man keeps quiet.

PROVERBS 29:11

400

O Lord, put a watch over my mouth. Keep watch over the door of my lips.

PSALM 141:3

Serving

God has called you to be a servant. You might be thinking, "Wait a minute? Am I supposed to be everyone's maid or waitress? How far does this servant thing go?" The truth is this: serving and loving go hand-in-hand. When you love someone, you want to care for them and make sure they have what they need. So don't chase after money or things. Don't be selfish. Live to serve others and you'll please God's heart.

401

"For the Son of Man did not come to be cared for. He came to care for others. He came to give His life so that many could be bought by His blood and be made free from sin."
MARK 10:45

402

God has given each of you a gift. Use it to help each other. This will show God's loving-favor.
1 PETER 4:10

403

"If you think it is wrong to serve the Lord, choose today whom you will serve. Choose the gods your fathers worshiped on the other side of the river, or choose the gods of the Amorites in whose land you are living. But as for me and my family, we will serve the Lord."
JOSHUA 24:15

404

Christian brother, you were chosen to be free. Be careful that you do not please your old selves by sinning because you are free. Live this free life by loving and helping others.
GALATIANS 5:13

405

"He who is greatest among you will be the one to care for you."
MATTHEW 23:11

406

Jesus sat down and called the followers to Him. He said, "If anyone wants to be first, he must be last of all. He will be the one to care for all."
MARK 9:35

407

"No one can have two bosses. He will hate the one and love the other. Or he will listen to the one and work against the other. You cannot have both God and riches as your boss at the same time."
MATTHEW 6:24

408

God always does what is right. He will not forget the work you did to help the Christians and the work you are still doing to help them. This shows your love for Christ.
HEBREWS 6:10

409

You obey the whole Law when you do this one thing, "Love your neighbor as you love yourself."
GALATIANS 5:14

410

Follow the Lord your God and fear Him. Keep His Laws, and listen to His voice. Work for Him, and hold on to Him.
DEUTERONOMY 13:4

Stand Strong

There are going to be days when you feel so weak that standing strong seems impossible. You'll just want to crawl into bed and pull the covers over your head. But even on those days, when things are really, really tough, God wants you to stand strong. Remember, it's His strength, not yours. So you can rest easy in Him!

411

Stand against him and be strong in your faith. Remember, other Christians over all the world are suffering the same as you are.
1 PETER 5:9

412

Watch and keep awake! Stand true to the Lord. Keep on acting like men and be strong.
1 CORINTHIANS 16:13

413

This is the last thing I want to say:
Be strong with the Lord's strength.
EPHESIANS 6:10

414

There is One Who can keep you from falling
and can bring you before Himself free from
all sin. He can give you great joy as you stand
before Him in His shining-greatness.
JUDE 1:24

415

Because of this, put on all the things God
gives you to fight with. Then you will be able
to stand in that sinful day. When it is all over,
you will still be standing.
EPHESIANS 6:13

416

Dear friends, if our heart does not say
that we are wrong, we will have no fear
as we stand before Him.
1 JOHN 3:21

417

So stand up and do not be moved. Wear a belt of truth around your body. Wear a piece of iron over your chest which is being right with God.
EPHESIANS 6:14

418

So lift up your hands that have been weak. Stand up on your weak legs.
HEBREWS 12:12

419

Live your lives as the Good News of Christ says you should. If I come to you or not, I want to hear that you are standing true as one. I want to hear that you are working together as one, preaching the Good News.
PHILIPPIANS 1:27

420

So give yourselves to God. Stand against the devil and he will run away from you.
JAMES 4:7

Temptation

Have you ever been tempted to do the wrong thing? Sure, everyone has! Some kids are tempted to cheat on a test. Others are tempted to overeat. Still others are tempted to hang out with kids who are bad influences. Jesus understands temptation. He was tempted by the devil. But guess what? He didn't give in to temptation. He has shown us that we don't have to give in either!

421

You have never been tempted to sin in any different way than other people. God is faithful. He will not allow you to be tempted more than you can take. But when you are tempted, He will make a way for you to keep from falling into sin.
1 Corinthians 10:13

422

"Watch and pray so that you will not be tempted. Man's spirit wants to do this, but the body does not have the power to do it."

MARK 14:38

423

When He got there, He said to them, "Pray that you will not be tempted."

LUKE 22:40

424

Christian brothers, if a person is found doing some sin, you who are stronger Christians should lead that one back into the right way. Do not be proud as you do it. Watch yourself, because you may be tempted also.

GALATIANS 6:1

425

When you are tempted to do wrong, do not say,
"God is tempting me." God cannot be tempted.
He will never tempt anyone.
JAMES 1:13

426

Because Jesus was tempted as we are and
suffered as we do, He understands us and He is
able to help us when we are tempted.
HEBREWS 2:18

427

A man is tempted to do wrong when he lets himself
be led by what his bad thoughts tell him to do.
JAMES 1:14

428

*Jesus was led by the Holy Spirit to a desert.
There He was tempted by the devil.*
MATTHEW 4:1

429

*But the Lord knows how to help men who are
right with God when they are tempted. He
also knows how to keep the sinners suffering
for their wrong-doing until the day they stand
before God Who will judge them.*
2 PETER 2:9

430

*A man who hurts people tempts his
neighbor to do the same, and leads him
in a way that is not good.*
PROVERBS 16:29

Thoughts

Did you know that God can read your mind? It's true! He knows your every thought—good and bad. That means He knows when you're in a bad mood and don't feel like obeying. He also knows when you're happy and content. God wants your thoughts to be more like His. You can be like Him by loving others and forgiving them—even when you think you're right. God promises to help you with this. Your thoughts matter, courageous girl!

431

Christian brothers, do not be like children in your thinking. Be full-grown, but be like children in not knowing how to sin.
1 CORINTHIANS 14:20

432

Follow my way of thinking as I follow Christ.
1 Corinthians 11:1

433

Christian brothers, keep your minds thinking about whatever is true, whatever is respected, whatever is right, whatever is pure, whatever can be loved, and whatever is well thought of. If there is anything good and worth giving thanks for, think about these things.
Philippians 4:8

434

"For My thoughts are not your thoughts, and My ways are not your ways," says the Lord.
Isaiah 55:8

435

Do not always be thinking about your own plans only. Be happy to know what other people are doing.
PHILIPPIANS 2:4

436

God's Word is living and powerful. It is sharper than a sword that cuts both ways. It cuts straight into where the soul and spirit meet and it divides them. It cuts into the joints and bones. It tells what the heart is thinking about and what it wants to do.
HEBREWS 4:12

437

My mouth will speak wisdom. And the thoughts of my heart will be understanding.
PSALM 49:3

438

Keep your minds thinking about things in heaven.
Do not think about things on the earth.
COLOSSIANS 3:2

439

Let the words of my mouth and the thoughts
of my heart be pleasing in Your eyes, O Lord,
my Rock and the One Who saves me.
PSALM 19:14

440

You know when I sit down and when I get up.
You understand my thoughts from far away.
PSALM 139:2

Trusting God

What does it mean to put your trust in someone? It means you're counting on them to do what they say. You hope they won't let you down. Unfortunately, people do let us down from time to time—it's part of being human. (Hey, even you have let people down a few times. . .right?) Would you like to know someone who will never let you down? You already do—it's Jesus! You can put all your trust in Him, and He will never break your heart. That's the best promise ever!

441

He will not be afraid of bad news. His heart is strong because he trusts in the Lord.
PSALM 112:7

442

Those who know Your name will put their trust in You. For You, O Lord, have never left alone those who look for You.
PSALM 9:10

443

The Lord is my strength and my safe cover. My heart trusts in Him, and I am helped. So my heart is full of joy. I will thank Him with my song.
PSALM 28:7

444

Trust in the Lord with all your heart, and do not trust in your own understanding.
PROVERBS 3:5

445

You will keep the man in perfect peace whose mind is kept on You, because he trusts in You.
ISAIAH 26:3

446

Trust in the Lord with all your heart, and do not trust in your own understanding. Agree with Him in all your ways, and He will make your paths straight.
PROVERBS 3:5–6

447

Good will come to the man who trusts in the Lord, and whose hope is in the Lord. He will be like a tree planted by the water, that sends out its roots by the river. It will not be afraid when the heat comes but its leaves will be green. It will not be troubled in a dry year, or stop giving fruit.
JEREMIAH 17:7–8

448

*It is better to trust in the Lord
than to trust in man.*
PSALM 118:8

449

*Give your way over to the Lord. Trust in
Him also. And He will do it.*
PSALM 37:5

450

When I am afraid, I will trust in You.
PSALM 56:3

Watching Your Words

What you say is important—whether you're talking to your friends, your parents, or your teachers. They care not only about what you say, but how you say it. Sure, sometimes you say the wrong thing. You get angry. You get sassy. But Jesus wants you to speak the way He does—with love, compassion, and truth. Keep a close eye on your words, courageous girl! They say a lot about who you are and who you serve.

451

Watch your talk! No bad words should be coming from your mouth. Say what is good. Your words should help others grow as Christians.
EPHESIANS 4:29

452

O Lord, put a watch over my mouth.
Keep watch over the door of my lips.
PSALM 141:3

453

My mouth will speak wisdom. And the thoughts
of my heart will be understanding.
PSALM 49:3

454

Death and life are in the power of the tongue,
and those who love it will eat its fruit.
PROVERBS 18:21

455

*My Christian brothers, you know everyone
should listen much and speak little. He should
be slow to become angry.*

JAMES 1:19

456

*A gentle answer turns away anger,
but a sharp word causes anger.*

PROVERBS 15:1

457

*With our tongue we give thanks to our Father in
heaven. And with our tongue we speak bad words
against men who are made like God. Giving thanks
and speaking bad words come from the same
mouth. My Christian brothers, this is not right!*

JAMES 3:9–10

458

He who watches over his mouth and his tongue keeps his soul from troubles.
PROVERBS 21:23

459

Pleasing words are like honey. They are sweet to the soul and healing to the bones.
PROVERBS 16:24

460

A gentle tongue is a tree of life, but a sinful tongue crushes the spirit.
PROVERBS 15:4

Wisdom

~~~~~~~~~~~~~~

Are wisdom and knowledge the same thing? Maybe you're book-smart, and you make straight A's. Does that make you wise? Here's the truth: wisdom is God-knowledge. This means you can't learn it in books. However, you can get it from hanging out with Jesus and learning to live the way He wants you to. So, here's the very best thing you can do: obtain knowledge (study your lessons) but get wisdom (from God and His Word) too. God promises to give it if you ask.

461

If you do not have wisdom, ask God for it.
He is always ready to give it to you and will
never say you are wrong for asking.
JAMES 1:5

462

Happy is the man who finds wisdom,
and the man who gets understanding. For it is
better than getting silver and fine gold.
PROVERBS 3:13-14

463

*Listen to words about what you should do,
and take your punishment if you need it,
so that you may be wise the rest of your days.*
PROVERBS 19:20

464

*The way of a fool is right in his own eyes,
but a wise man listens to good teaching.*
PROVERBS 12:15

465

*For the Lord gives wisdom. Much learning
and understanding come from His mouth.*
PROVERBS 2:6

466

*For I will give you wisdom in what to say
and I will help you say it. Those who are
against you will not be able to stop you
or say you are wrong.*
LUKE 21:15

467

The fear of the Lord is the beginning of much learning. Fools hate wisdom and teaching.
PROVERBS 1:7

468

The fear of the Lord is the beginning of wisdom. To learn about the Holy One is understanding.
PROVERBS 9:10

469

The beginning of wisdom is: Get wisdom! And with all you have gotten, get understanding.
PROVERBS 4:7

470

"Whoever hears these words of Mine and does them, will be like a wise man who built his house on rock."
MATTHEW 7:24

Witness

If you discovered a medicine that would cure the deadliest disease, would you tell people about it? If you found a million dollars in a field, would you share the news with those you love? Sure you would! When you have exciting news to tell, you don't hold anything back. Here's a fun fact: you already have the best news there is! Jesus is the Savior of the world. Don't hold back. Let everyone know!

471

"Let your light shine in front of men. Then they will see the good things you do and will honor your Father Who is in heaven."
MATTHEW 5:16

472

"But you will receive power when the Holy Spirit comes into your life. You will tell about Me in the city of Jerusalem and over all the countries of Judea and Samaria and to the ends of the earth."
ACTS 1:8

473

Then I heard the voice of the Lord, saying,
"Whom should I send? Who will go for Us?"
Then I said, "Here am I. Send me!"
Isaiah 6:8

474

I am not ashamed of the Good News. It is the
power of God. It is the way He saves men from the
punishmentof their sins if they put their trust in Him.
It is for the Jew first and for all other people also.
Romans 1:16

475

He put a new song in my mouth, a song of
praise to our God. Many will see and fear
and will put their trust in the Lord.
Psalm 40:3

476

Do not be ashamed to tell others about what our Lord
said, or of me here in prison. I am here because of
Jesus Christ. Be ready to suffer for preaching the Good
News and God will give you the strength you need.
2 Timothy 1:8

477

"Go and make followers of all the nations. Baptize them in the name of the Father and of the Son and of the Holy Spirit. Teach them to do all the things I have told you. And I am with you always, even to the end of the world."

MATTHEW 28:19–20

478

"You can speak for Me," says the Lord. "You are My servant whom I have chosen so that you may know and believe Me, and understand that I am He. No God was made before Me, and there will be none after Me."

ISAIAH 43:10

479

"And when I am lifted up from the earth, I will attract all people toward Me."

JOHN 12:32

480

"This Good News about the holy nation of God must be preached over all the earth. It must be told to all nations and then the end will come."

MATTHEW 24:14

Worry

When you're worried, who do you talk to? Jesus promises to take your worries if you'll just give them to Him. No matter what you're upset about—your grades, a friendship, or your relationship with your parents, you can go straight to Him. The Lord promises to take those worries and give you the faith you need to get through the situation. All you need to do is pray and ask Him to help you. And in that moment, His peace will wash over you.

481

Do not worry. Learn to pray about everything. Give thanks to God as you ask Him for what you need. The peace of God is much greater than the human mind can understand. This peace will keep your hearts and minds through Christ Jesus.

PHILIPPIANS 4:6–7

482

*Give all your worries to Him
because He cares for you.*
1 PETER 5:7

483

*"I tell you this: Do not worry about your
life. Do not worry about what you are
going to eat and drink. Do not worry about
what you are going to wear. Is not life
more important than food? Is not the body
more important than clothes?"*
MATTHEW 6:25

484

*Worry in the heart of a man weighs it down,
but a good word makes it glad.*
PROVERBS 12:25

485

"Do not worry about tomorrow. Tomorrow will have its own worries. The troubles we have in a day are enough for one day."

MATTHEW 6:34

486

"Peace I leave with you. My peace I give to you. I do not give peace to you as the world gives. Do not let your hearts be troubled or afraid."

JOHN 14:27

487

Give all your cares to the Lord and He will give you strength. He will never let those who are right with Him be shaken.

PSALM 55:22

488

"Do not let your heart be troubled. You have put
your trust in God, put your trust in Me also."
JOHN 14:1

489

"Which of you can make yourself
a little taller by worrying?"
LUKE 12:25

490

Jesus said to His followers, "Because of this,
I say to you, do not worry about your life, what
you are going to eat. Do not worry about your
body, what you are going to wear."
LUKE 12:22

You're One of a Kind

~~~~~~~~~~

There's no one on planet earth just like you. No one has your smile, your freckles, your fingerprint, or your exact personality. You are truly one of a kind, courageous girl! And God wants you to celebrate your uniqueness. Don't worry about fitting in. Don't try to be like anyone else. You just be you. . .and enjoy every moment!

491

I will give thanks to You, for the greatness of the way I was made brings fear. Your works are great and my soul knows it very well.
PSALM 139:14

492

"Before I started to put you together in your mother, I knew you. Before you were born, I set you apart as holy. I chose you to speak to the nations for Me."

JEREMIAH 1:5

493

We are His work. He has made us to belong to Christ Jesus so we can work for Him. He planned that we should do this.

EPHESIANS 2:10

494

God knows how many hairs you have on your head.

MATTHEW 10:30

495

*" 'For I know the plans I have for you,' says the
Lord, 'plans for well-being and not for trouble,
to give you a future and a hope.' "*
JEREMIAH 29:11

496

*But now, O Lord, You are our Father.
We are the clay, and You are our pot maker.
All of us are the work of Your hand.*
ISAIAH 64:8

497

*For You made the parts inside me.
You put me together inside my mother.*
PSALM 139:13

498

*But the Lord said to Samuel, "Do not look
at the way he looks on the outside or how tall
he is, because I have not chosen him. For the
Lord does not look at the things man looks at.
A man looks at the outside of a person,
but the Lord looks at the heart."*
1 Samuel 16:7

499

*The Holy Spirit has been given to you
and you all know the truth.*
1 John 2:20

500

*There are many people who belong to Christ.
And yet, we are one body which is Christ's.
We are all different but we depend on each other.*
Romans 12:5

More Books for Courageous Girls!

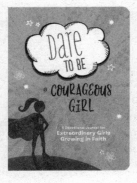

Dare to Be a Courageous Girl

This delightfully unique journal will challenge courageous girls like you to live boldly for God! With each turn of the page, you will encounter a new "dare" from the easy-to-understand New Life Version of scripture alongside a brief devotional reading and thought-provoking journal prompt or "challenge" that encourages you to take action and obey God's Word.

Paperback / 978-1-64352-642-3 / $14.99

Choose Extraordinary

Be encouraged to live an extraordinary life for God with these 180 devotions and prayers. Each reading will challenge you to be courageous in faith like dozens of Bible heroines including Esther, Hannah, Mary, Ruth, the Woman Who Needed Healing, and more—while you come to know and understand how to be courageous too! Be captured by truth, adventure, and Bible heroines galore!

Paperback / 978-1-64352-803-8 / $4.99